CURVES OF THE SOUL

Blanca Urquhart

CURVES OF THE SOUL

eclipsa

Editorial Eclipsa
editorial@casadcarton.es
www.eclipsa.com.es

First edition: April 2014

ISBN: 978-84-941240-4-4
Depósito Legal: M-17085-2014

Printed in Spain
Imprenta Prin House

For all the Dragonesses who live inside us.
For all those women who are sinners and saints, to
those who are faithful and adulterous.
Those submissive and those who have voice, to the
mothers and wives, lovers,
daughters, sisters, cousins and friends.
To all those who feel loved and alone.
To those who hide themselves and the ones who show
themselves in the daylight.
To those who still believe in love, passion and romance.
To those who have lost direction in life and are seeking
the path.
To the worrior women
and those who are learning to be so.
To those who feel suffocated and want to scream.
To all of those who are Goddesses and Dragonesses,
but have yet to realize.

I like nonsense, it wakes up the brain cells.
Fantasy is a necessary ingredient in living;
it's a way of looking at life through
the wrong end of a telescope.
Which is what I do, and that enables
you to laugh at life's realities.

DR. SEUSS

The woman who follows the crowd
will usually go no further than the crowd.
The woman that walks alone is likely
to find herself in places no one has been before.

ALBERT EINSTEIN

Perhaps

I have never been an academic woman,
which is perhaps why I always smile.
I have never been an elegant woman,
which is probably why I am always comfortable.
I have never been a judgmental woman,
which is perhaps why I am so free.
I have never been competitive,
which is perhaps why I always excel in something.
I have never been a beautiful woman,
but my body is accentuated with curves and valleys
and my eye-piercing gaze has been a magical spell
for many men in my life.
I have never been overly intelligent, but my words have
always been sought after and listened to.
I have never been one to ask for much,
but I am surprised that I have it all.
I have never been severe, which is probably
why those who are, seek my company.
I have never trusted many, but very few times in life
I have been betrayed.
I have never been an envious woman,
which is perhaps why I have so many friends.
I have never had many goals,
but have obtained almost everything I want in life.
I have never been an inquisitive woman,
which may be why fortune smiles on me.
I have never been spiteful,
which is probably why I forget so easily.
I have never wanted to be a perfect woman,
which is perhaps why I often surprise people.
I have never expected others to love me,
which might be the reason I find love all the time.
I have never been a submissive woman,
which is perhaps, just perhaps,
why I can write these words.

I forgive myself

I forgive myself for all the times I let myself be vanquished by the comfort of saying no.

I forgive myself for all the times I put others first and sacrificed my own wellbeing.

I forgive myself for the sins I committed on behalf of trying to attain the "good life".

I forgive myself for not listening to my own thoughts.

I forgive myself for all those wasted nights trying to forget you.

I forgive myself for the countless times I felt guilty without reason.

I forgive myself for having forgotten all my dreams.

I forgive myself for being a coward before all the injustices I witnessed.

I forgive myself for all the hurtful words I let you speak to me.

I forgive myself for all the times I did not love you.

I forgive myself for all the nights with the full moon that I did not howl.

I forgive myself for hiding my feelings in the darkness of my soul.

I forgive myself for being blind to the light of freedom.

I forgive myself for having encaged myself without need.

I forgive myself a thousand times, for crying alone.

I forgive myself for the moments I did not enjoy.

I forgive myself for acting happy instead of letting myself feel sadness.

I forgive myself for the occasions that I hid and did not defend myself.

I forgive myself for the lost years between the broom and the dishes.

I forgive myself for all the invitations to sin that I rejected.

I forgive myself for all those Saturday nights I did not dance.

I forgive myself for forgetting that I am a beautiful, powerful woman. I will never let myself forget.

when I was in Paris was wanting
I was expecting - instead they were
not unlike others.
we took the train to
Pamplona. We spent two days in
Fiesta de San Fermin
and the city never sleeps.

A mother's love

What could I, as a mother, say to you, my daughter? What would be the only sublime message that could be forever etched in your soul as a woman? Your mother, a woman like many others, my daughter, a woman like many others.

Woman, my daughter, my shadow, my creation, my hopes, my gift, my religion. Woman, my daughter, what advice can I give you as your mother?

I love you and protect you with a love that has no boundaries, no beginning and no end, and will sacrifice everything for you. I love you because you are part of me. I love you because you are who I am and am not; I adore you because you're my past, my present and my future. I cherish you because I've always felt that way; I love you because there is no other way. My daughter, the woman you are, the woman you will be, the woman of long ago.

Life will teach you, life will guide you, people will criticize you, your soul will break, joy will surprise you, tears will run, love will blind you, suffering will attack you, life will amaze you. Your mother will be with you.

Passion, love, desire, carefree adventure, romance, complicity, cuddling, desire, insanity, instinct, compassion, illusions, everything without limits. Let yourself be tempted, let yourself be invited, let yourself be taken, abandon yourself to feelings, let yourself be adored, let yourself be touched, let romance into your heart, let yourself be worshiped, accept help, be a heroine, abandon yourself to be part of stories and adventures, be pampered, protected, just let yourself go… because the time will come, daughter of my soul, when only memories will accompany you, images from the past will make you smile, and that which you have experienced and everything you have lived will make you wise.

Life's magic will appear before you whenever you are a sorceress; love will be part of you whenever you let yourself go unconditionally; freedom will be your twin if you do not build a prison.

Fly with the wings of youth, without fear, without borders. Never learn what limits mean.

Thanks

I am grateful I was born in the wrong country,with the history and culture of the Inquisition inherited from our conquerors because it gave me the wings to fly far away.

I am thankful I have been criticized for being different, because it taught me to listen to my spirit and avoid jerks.

I am thankful for so many restrictions, because it pushed me to be creative.

I am thankful for my round, curvy body from days gone by because it has been desired and loved.

I appreciate the tenderness of my first lover, because he taught me to surrender to love fearlessly.

I am thankful I didn't have it all, because it made me grateful.

I am thankful for suffering, because it showed me the way to happiness.

I am grateful for that wonderful man who cannot resist my wide hips, because he taught me to dress differently.

I am thankful for those moments of happiness that engraved the smile on my lips.

I am thankful for my daughters who taught me the meaning of unconditional love.

I am thankful for the strong arms that have sheltered me, because they taught me to trust.

I am thankful for my instinct, because it taught me that I could do the impossible.

I am thankful for the fiery passion of desire, because it made me a woman.

I appreciate so very much the man who touched my skin and turned me into Aphrodite.

I have to give thanks for being born without guilt because it opened the road to sin.

I am thankful for being distracted because I don't notice when someone does me wrong.

I am thankful for my partner for forgetting I am his wife when he takes me to bed and I become his lover.

Above all, I give thanks to life that has given me so much and more.

I am thankful… I am grateful… to be a woman.

How can I forget?

Memories get confused with my very real and ordinary days, and my desires fade with routine chores, my exhausted body sleeps without feelings, without needs, without memories.

Your image appeared like lightning, your scent possessed me. Instinct woke inside me and violently invaded my being, quickly, without questioning, inadvertently, without searching.

Forgetting on the other hand is slow, as much as I would like to, memories permeate my thoughts, the feel of your touch on my body still consumes me and your tastes still lie on my mouth.

Your absence is stronger than your presence. Forgetting is rebellious; it won't be left behind, nor persuaded.

How slow time passes when melancholy is your partner; how fast time passed when you were with me.

I can't help but remember, I cannot help feeling; I can't help but see you're gone; forgetfulness has betrayed me. It has not arrived, even though I call out for it incessantly.

The minute hand is stuck on the clock, the hours do not advance, the days are endless and your image continues to sneak through my head. I cannot stop thinking of you, your presence will not leave me even though you want nothing more to do with mine.

I know

I know you no longer love me, because your hands
  no longer brush mine as you walk by me.
I know you no longer see me, because
  my reflection is not in your eyes.
I know you no longer think of me
  when you don't call during the day.
I know you forgot my body when
  your hands do not recognize it.
I know you no longer feel me when
  you don't kiss me at night.
I know you no longer dream of me
  when you don't seek me in bed.
I know I am no longer desirable to you
  because you don't look at me when I undress.
I know you are forgetting me
  when you don't call me by my name.
I know my words tire you when you don't respond.
I know you no longer hear my sobs when I am next to you.
I know you no longer have fun with me
  because you do not smile.
I know your desire has died
  because I no longer feel you inside of me.
I know you are thinking of another
  because your absence tells me so.
I know you will not stay because you are not present now.
I know I let you go a while back but I didn't know it.
I know you no longer need me because you don't ask for me.
I know I am not familiar to you
  because you distance yourself from me.
I know you prefer solitude
  because you don't look for my company.
I know that love has died
  because all I do now is think about it.
I know the only thing left between us is history.
I know you had told me this, but I had forgotten.

Tomorrow

Tomorrow, I will come back to you. Tomorrow, I will go back to the life that I chose long ago. To the life of security, rules, and formality. But today, I'm staying here, with him.

Tomorrow, I'll be myself again. The one that loves you, the one that listens to you, the one that's always there…But today, I remain dreaming in his arms. Today, I run from the life that is awaiting me and seek refuge in his kisses.

Tomorrow is another day. Tomorrow, I will be by your side as you wish, but today I will be different. Today, I will be the one who loves and is loved by another, the one who sleeps peacefully atop the naked body of another. Today, I will be the one that doesn't want to think that you'll be waiting for me.

Tomorrow, I will dress the way you like me to dress, but today, I will remove my clothes and loosen my hair. Today, I will be indecent and I will smile because I am with him. Tomorrow will be another day, another beginning. Tomorrow, you'll receive me with happiness because you need me, because you're expecting me. Tomorrow, I will pretend I am happy, tomorrow I will spend hours washing off his scent so my body gets used to being without him so I can cool my soul from so much love.

But today, I am here with him, I take his hand, I smell his neck, I kiss his mouth, I feel him inside of me, I capture his silhouette, the groans, the words. I engrave in my hands the curves of his body, I collect the aromas that emanate from inside of him. Today is now, today is the present, today is what I am, and the memory that allows me to return to what I do not want.

Tomorrow, I will think about staying with you because tomorrow… perhaps… you will be him.

Sin

It would be a sin if I did not let myself be taken away by
the attraction of being with you.
It would be a sin if I didn't pay attention
to the desires
that burn within me every time I think of you.
It would be a crime if I did not kiss you every time
I see you.
It would be a sin if I were not to enjoy your body
every time I have you next to me
and an even greater sin if I did not let myself
be consumed by the fire that your touch
desperately provokes in me.

I would be converted into a sinner
if I did not let you enter me every time
you desired, an offense to not taste
you when you are in my mouth.
It would be a crime if I did not let your fingers enter me.
A sinner, I would be, if I did not allow your tongue
to calm my body's hunger, a liar if I didn't repeat
over and over that I want more of you.
I would be banished to hell if I didn't allow your eyes
to hypnotize me, to take me to heaven every time you
possess me. I know paradise only because
your body shows me every time you leave me
exhausted from so much feeling.

I feel despair every time you brush me
with your hands without touching me completely.
It would be a sin if I did not hear your groans
when you are making love to me.
I would be a delinquent if I did not let myself
be bewithced by your aroma.
What a terrible sin it would be if I did not unleash the
storm of lust I feel when anticipating our encounters.

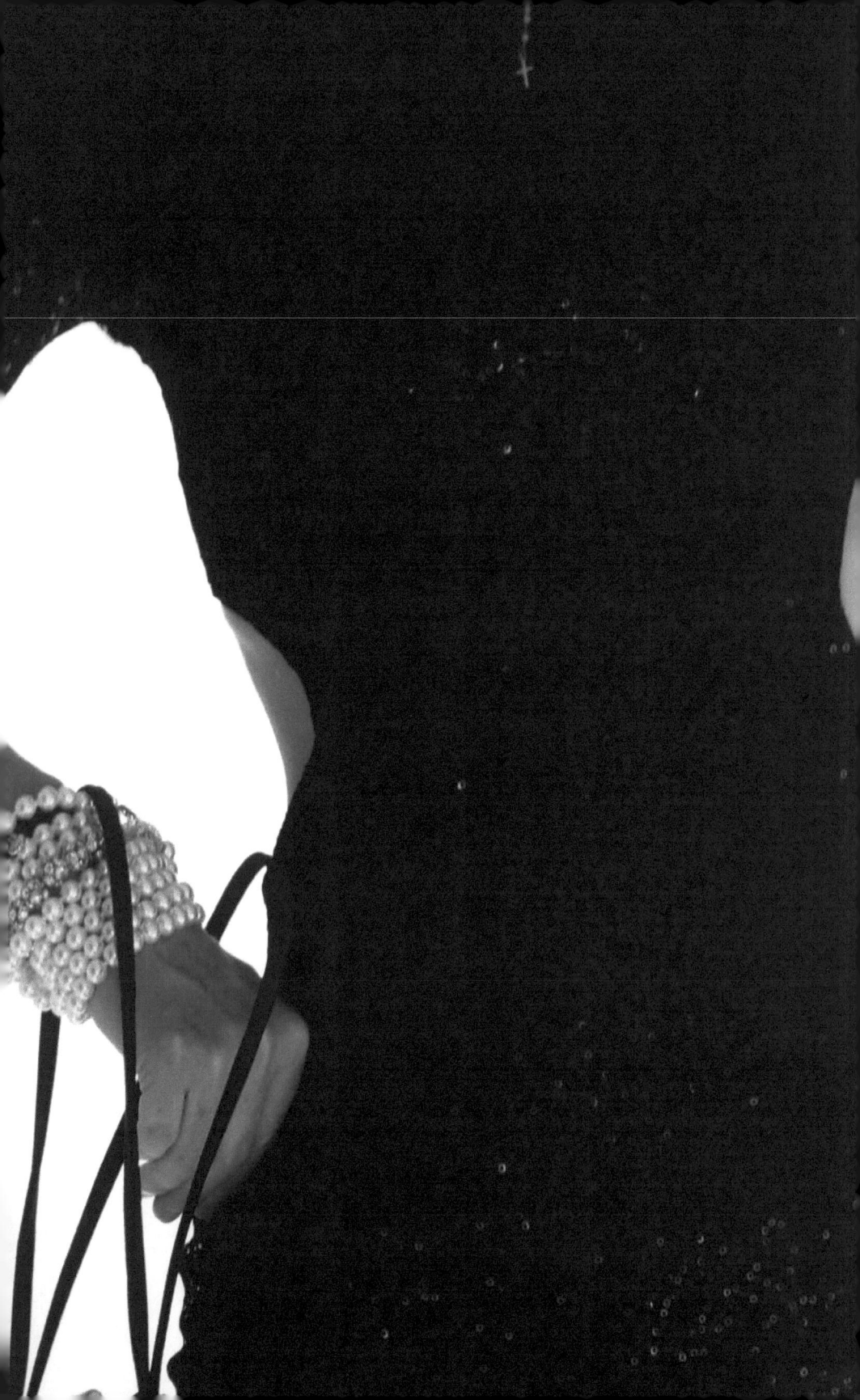

I have communion with God every time
your body and mine become one.
Whispers become requests for more.
The exuberance of my body is the sin
that provokes you, the spasms of our souls
are the unification of everything and more.
It would be a sin if I wasn't a sinner.

I want to be

I don't want to see the rain through the window.
I want to be the rain and soak your body.
I don't want to feel the fire of the logs in front of me.
I want to be the fire that burns your soul.
I am through with reading love stories,
I want to be the protagonist,
I want my own hero, my own prince, my own lover,
my own story.
I don't want to watch any more adventure movies,
I want to be the heroine, the one that suffers from
bewitched passions and fights with dragons.
I'm through with listening to stories of impossible loves,
I want to live them, I want to feel them,
I want to suffer them, I want to immortalize them.
I don't mind going straight to hell
if that would allow me to impregnate myself
with prohibited passions, tenebrous, dark, forbidden,
all that is not allowed.
I don't care if I don't see heaven,
if I can satiate myself with your body,
with your hands burning mine, with your tounge
discovering every one of my corners.
I am O.K. with being a sinner
as long as I can be your lover forever.
I am not afraid of meeting the devil himself
if I can feel my mouth filling with you,
if I can feed off of your kisses, your hugs, your glance,
your touch, your everything…
I don't care if you mind,
because I don't care about anything if you are not here.

I'm leaving

I'm leaving you because I don't want pieces of you. I'm leaving because I need more. I'm leaving because your glance no longer retains me. I'm leaving because your kisses no longer open my mouth. I'm going because your hands no longer touch me. I'm leaving because your words sound empty. I'm going because your body no longer warms me. I'm leaving because you no longer hear my cries. I'm going because my soul is getting cold. I'm leaving because you no longer care about me. I'm going because I can't conform. I'm leaving because I no longer make you laugh. I'm leaving because your arms no longer rock me at night. I'm leaving because I no longer want to be ignored. I'm going because you're clipping my wings. I'm leaving because I am not myself when I'm with you. I'm going because you don't want me by your side. I'm leaving because it's what my intuition tells me. I'm going because I don't want to be a ghost. I'm leaving because when we make love, I don't feel anything anymore. I'm going because my passion no longer provokes you. I'm leaving because you no longer touch my body. I'm going because you no longer look at me. I'm leaving because I'm searching for lust. I'm going because I don't want to be alone anymore. I'm leaving because I want to be full of love. I'm going because I desire passion. I'm leaving because you're no longer with me. I'm leaving because I want to be the only one. I'm going because I no longer love you. I'm leaving because I bore you. I'm going because your denial tells me to. I'm leaving because I'm no longer with you. I'm going because my spirit has already left. I'm leaving because I believe in miracles. I'm leaving so I can feel free. I'm going because I can. I'm leaving because I can't stay. I'm going with a smile. I'm going because I'm drowning. I'm leaving because I don't know what else to do. I leave you and I go happy.

Fear

Fear paralyzes me, it consumes me. The fear of losing you, of making a mistake, of being without you. Decisions get confused with the rational, with emotions with memories, with the conventional and the uncertain. Bravery vanishes when you are not sure, when the unknown waits outside. Choice is difficult when the soul is cold, the spirit low, the thoughts murky. Weariness is present in the soul, tears do not cease to fall, words are no longer pronounced, sight no longer wants to see.

Habit is all present, routine does not allow you to see with clarity, the history that you and I wrote, it cannot find the last chapter. It stayed in the past without moving forward. I am without being, you look at me without seeing, you speak to me without me listening, you hug me as usual, I say I love you because it's what I've been saying for centuries.

I go far, I distance myself, I protect myself, I leave and I'm still here, always here, waiting. I postponed myself for tomorrow. A tomorrow that never arrives. I trick myself in order to carry out the present, I dream of what I can't have. I'm frozen by cowardliness. I die slowly every day for fear of being alone, of ghosts that will leave with me.

The lost illusion of love consumes me little by little, the incomprehension of wanting to be understood erases me, the idealism of the romantic disillusions me, the reason for living evaporates and only melancholy remains.

Fear is stuck to my skin, it weakens me, it makes me a docile being. That fear is the reason I haven't left. That fear is the reason I stay. That fear makes me one more of the many cowards that walk around everywhere wearing a smiling mask.

Words

The unspoken words are the ones that suffocate me.
The words that don't come from my mouth are
those that block the soul. The words I utter
that don't find a response are those that make me cry.
So many words unspoken are
the ones that make me forget how to speak.
Those half-finished sentences are the ones
that distance us; the uncomfortable silences are the ones
that speak your words loudly.
Your repetitive stories are the ones
which make me distance myself from you.
Your meaningless words leave me silent.
Cold.
The discussions about others are the ones
that silence our own. It is the monotone
of your voice that tells me to go.
The feelings in my mouth are the ones which scare you.
The words you spend on another
which aren't there for me.
The words I whisper to another
which you do not want to hear.
Your passionless voice disillusions me...
It is my conversation that is full of life
the one that kills yours.

And so it is...

And so it is… as you once told me, gifts arrive when you least expect them; they appear out of nowhere, when you are not seeking them. This is how I found you, without searching for you, without even thinking of you. This is how we recognized each other. Our bodies knew our story before we even touched.

This is how I found myself in your arms. This is how your kisses woke in me what had been asleep for so long. Your hands sculpted my body once again and your words created an enchanting fairytale of old.

And so it is… things happen because they are written in our destiny. Love arrives when one isn't seeking it. Passion takes over when you have forgotten what it feels like. This is how I began to realize that love snatches away all reason and passion leaves you without thoughts and only feelings.

This is how, without wanting to find you, I found you. I, who was thinking that love was no longer possible, who could no longer remember that my body could feel. Wise destiny guided me to your smile, your eyes. I tied myself to your body as if we had always been joined together. This is how you also came to me, in the same way, without wanting to find me, without wanting to discover me… without thinking that I was there. Without knowing…

And so it is… Today, I wake in the middle of the night, asking myself if it was real or just a dream…I close my eyes and feel your hands caressing my body. This is how you said it would be. The taste of kisses cannot be erased, cannot be washed away, cannot be taken. This is how I left you, with the strength of your mouth on mine, your handprints on my body. This is why I no longer want to be here, if you are not here with me, since I can no longer feel if not with you.

And so it is… I still feel your warm breath on my neck. This is how I fade little by little without your hands in mine, without your whispers in my ear. This is how, with the passing of time, as you said would happen, your words become distorted and dim in the fading light. This is how I ask myself if you are with her now, if you still love her.

And so it is... I recall you told me one day it would be, that as love can arrive without warning, you also have to beg to let it go. And so it is, I write even though I know you won't read my letters. I have no tears left. I am spent. This is how your memory haunts me day and night as I reach out for your body during the long night and feel only the pain that was left.

And so it is... I became a poet, and what was important before, now has no meaning. This is why my body no longer feels others' hands, my eyes no longer shine with breathless anticipation, and my hands no longer caress another's body. And so it is, I spend more time in dreams than in reality, in places where I can see your smile and breathe in the sunshine of your scent. Will I ever be free?

And so it is... as you said it would be, but is not. Each of us left to travel our own worlds. The memories of your body inside mine have never left me, your smile is still engraved on my mind, your kisses linger on my mouth and I am no longer who I used to be.

This is how I became addicted to you. I need you so I can breathe and you are not here. This is how I cannot understand why I have not been able to let you go. I don't know if it was God or the devil that sent you to me. I don't want to ask for fear you'll never return.

And so it is... as you told me it would be, why I still believe in miracles and hope to see you amongst the people walking towards me.

And so it is... I know I will never feel your touch again, that my eyes will never see yours again. I know. But, I don't know the difference between love and passion, craziness and reason.

And so it is... I cease to be whole when I'm not with you. But that's the way it will be, as you said it would be... When I don't expect you, when I don't think of you, when I don't feel you... perhaps I will see you again.

The Dragoness

My wings were broken. I discovered this the day I wanted to fly. The day that I remembered I had them was too late; the wings that were always with me were no longer there. The wings that made me free had vanished, leaving me a prisoner of the earth, taking away the vision of other worlds, the clear skies, the bright stars, the mystic and silent nights. Nobody stole them from me, nobody asked to borrow them. The lack of use simply destroyed them.

So much time spent keeping busy, going from one place to the next, so many years anchored to the reality of daily routine, so many lives given for other lives, so many efforts to fulfill dreams that didn't belong to me. My wings were left between faded sheets, bright pots and dirty brooms. And what is a Dragoness without her wings?

The ferocity of my personality vanished, my free spirit overcome with the mundane, the passionate fire that would come from my mouth with words of love was slowly extinguished, giving ground to cold disillusion and conformity. Nobody put out the fire I had inside of me. I simply forgot how to feel it, neglecting it with so much human work that it confused the memory. It vanished with so many rules and judgments and I could no longer determine what was right or wrong. And now I'm alone without belonging to this world or the other. And so what does a woman do to reclaim her Dragoness?

I don't care

I don't care what people say about me, I'm not worried that people fill their days with conversations about my leaving.

I could care less that nobody understands that I left because I had to go, that the air was heavy, breathing was difficult, that I couldn't continue lying, that I had no option.

I understand that people cannot conceive what I feel for you, I don't care if they criticize me because I know that not everyone can submerge themselves in the passion which I find myself.

It's not relevant if the life I had yesterday has been destroyed, the joy I had before you has no meaning because today I feel happiness in abundance only because I'm here, with you. It doesn't affect me if people are right when they tell me that I will be sorry, because I know I will suffer, I don't care if I'm dead to him because I started to truly live when I left his side.

I don't care what my values were because I left them behind and adopted new ones. I don't care if I am drugged with your scent because I feel great, I don't care if I am bewitched by your words because I like their sound, I don't care if they tell me I'm crazy because I know it's true.

I don't care about anything, only your presence next to mine, your look sustaining mine, your arms hugging me at night and knowing that you do care that I love you.

Absence

So much was left unsaid, so many words that were confused in the rush of the moment, so much you simply never knew about me, so much I never had the chance to know about you. So many years together, so many memories, so much history, so much love, so much complicity.

I read somewhere, that melancholy can take hold of the feelings of those left alone, of those in mourning, of those who have lost something vital in their lives. This is how I'm feeling, sad, lonely, melancholy. Always thinking of you, always wanting to feel your hand in mine once again, wanting to smile, even if it were the last time I saw you asleep next to me. Melancholy takes me to the place where everything used to be, where warmth and comfort sheltered my soul.

My body grows cold without your body at night. Even my tears don't fall; I exhausted them all. Your things remind me you will never return. Your scent lingers and I am unable to stop calling out for you, to ask you to return… even for a brief moment. I seek you during moments of happiness; I need you during times of weakness. My soul aches for my loss. I am unable to kiss you again, I am broken inside and I do not care, I want to go, as well. I want to disappear, because I no longer know how to live without you beside me.

You left without warning…unwittingly, in a hurry, with pain, and only now do I forgive you. Now I know there are things in life that cannot be turned back, now I know you are waiting for me in another place and that death is not an abandonment, but rather a step further to a place of a happy reunion.

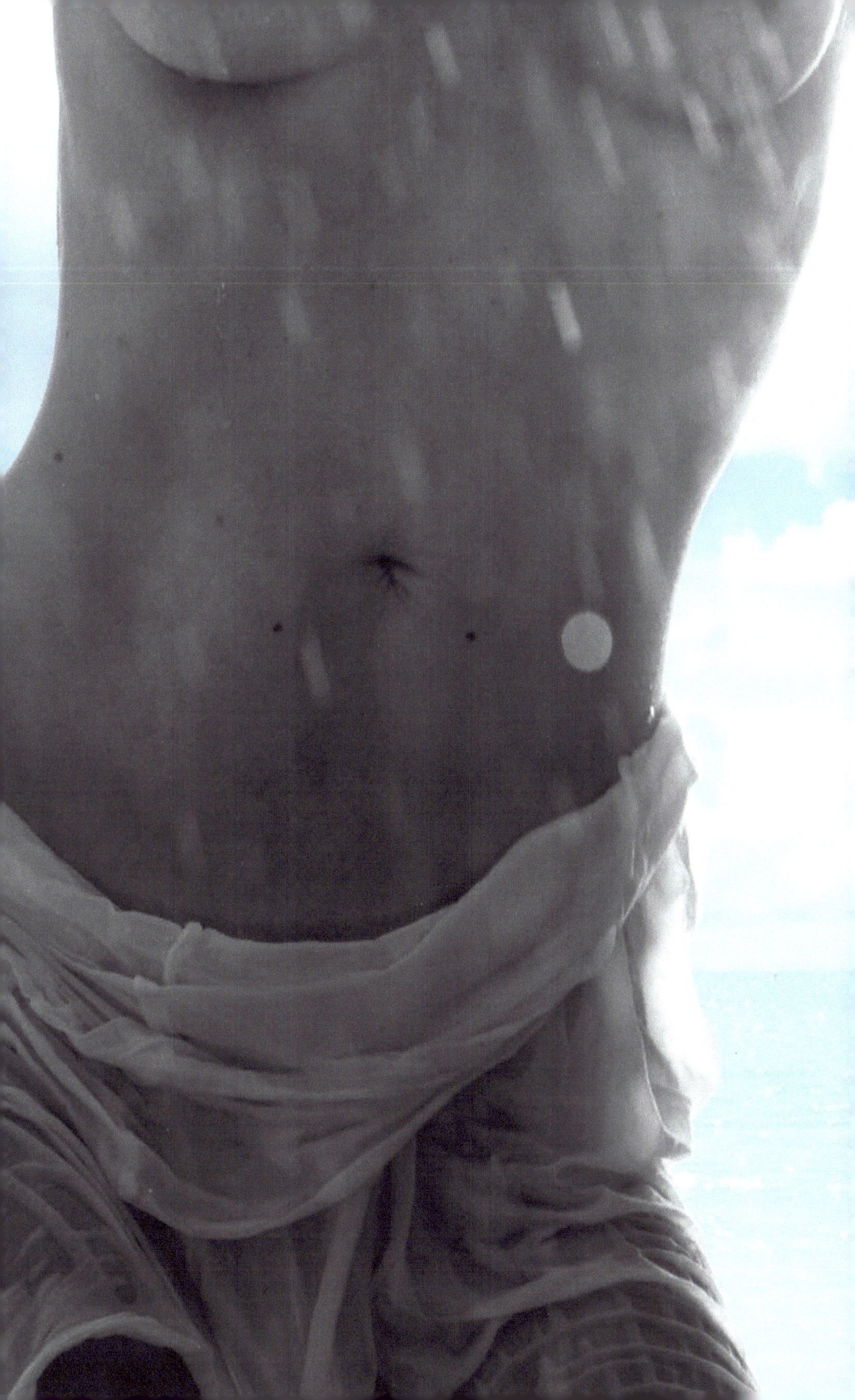

The foreboding

I could feel it when I was in your presence,
I knew deep inside me, when walking next to you…
your words told me. I knew when I asked your name…
I knew when your hand touched mine.
I could tell when I looked in your eyes,
sensed it when you sat next to me…
I knew when awake in the middle of the night,
I knew from the moment I met you,
and I confirmed it when you looked at me.
I felt it when you touched me…
Dreams told me and I knew.
I reconfirmed everything when I saw you again.
I knew calmly when I told you, blushed when you
smiled, sensed it when you spoke to me.
I discovered it when you walked towards me.
I accepted it when you agreed. I knew when
I crossed the bridge. I wanted it when I touched you,
I desired it when you kissed me, I wanted it when
I looked at you. I felt the passion when I dreamed of you,
I smelled you when you were next to me,
I tasted you when I entered your mouth,
I shuddered when you hugged me,
I forgot the world when you stripped me.
I surrendered myself with your tongue between my legs.
You made me part of you forever with your gaze. I loved
you when you were inside of me. I felt your absence when
you departed my side…
And now… I call out for you when you are not here.
I need you every minute, I think of you night and day,
my body desires yours, my mouth is parched without yours.
My hands outline your body, my dreams scream out for you.
I haven't forgotten you with time. I always knew I would
suffer.

With him

I like to be with you because of how you make me feel,
and for what I become when I'm next to you.
You have the power to make me feel infinite,
and my thoughts to vanish. I love to be with you
because you only know the woman that
I want you to see, I'm fascinated with being by your side
and letting my animal instincts be free,
my cavewoman-like intuition.
I love when I have no decency nor consciousness,
I don't tie myself to social convictions.
I am a woman, I am desire, I am passion.
I am who I am. I am lust, I am instinct,
I am procreation. I am pleasure. I am sin.
I am everything I am not.
I'm overwhelmed with how much
I'm able to enjoy when I have you near me,
I wrap myself in what my body feels,
you turn me into what I was centuries ago.
You recognized me from the beginning even before
I knew who I was. I'm enchanted
by the delight of touching you,
I love to feel that I am who I think I am not.
You next to me…My legs bringing your body closer
to mine. My tongue in your mouth searching
for that mystery of eternal life. Your hands climbing
my thighs in desperate search of a lost paradise.
Your scent of a man from times gone by,
that scent that mixes with mine
which comes from inside,
those scents that only lovers recognize,
scents that awaken senses.
I love what your starving hands
can awaken inside of me,
I'm satisfied when my body shakes
with the feeling of your fingers inside of me.
I am delighted in the havoc you provoke
with your soft kisses on my breasts,

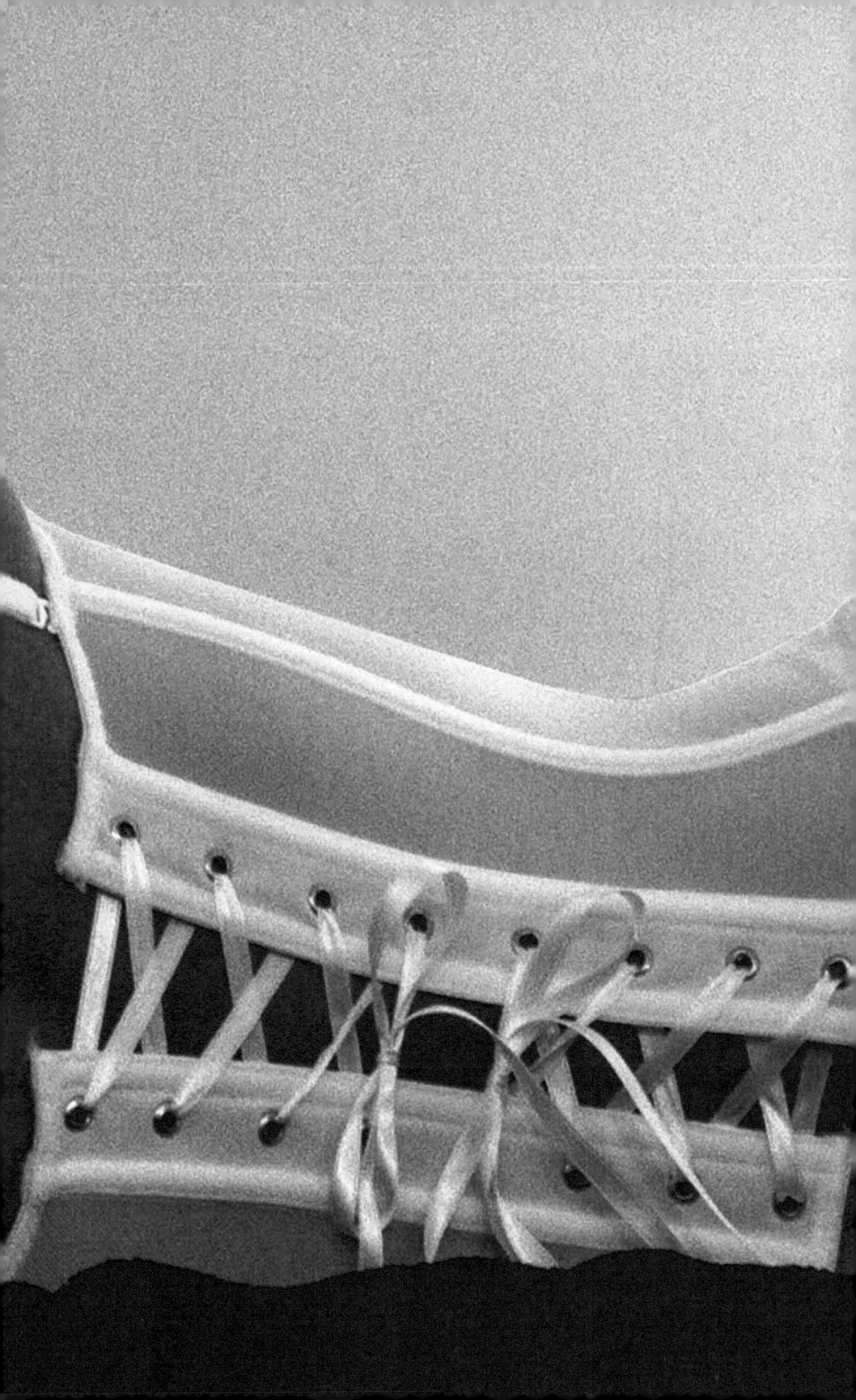

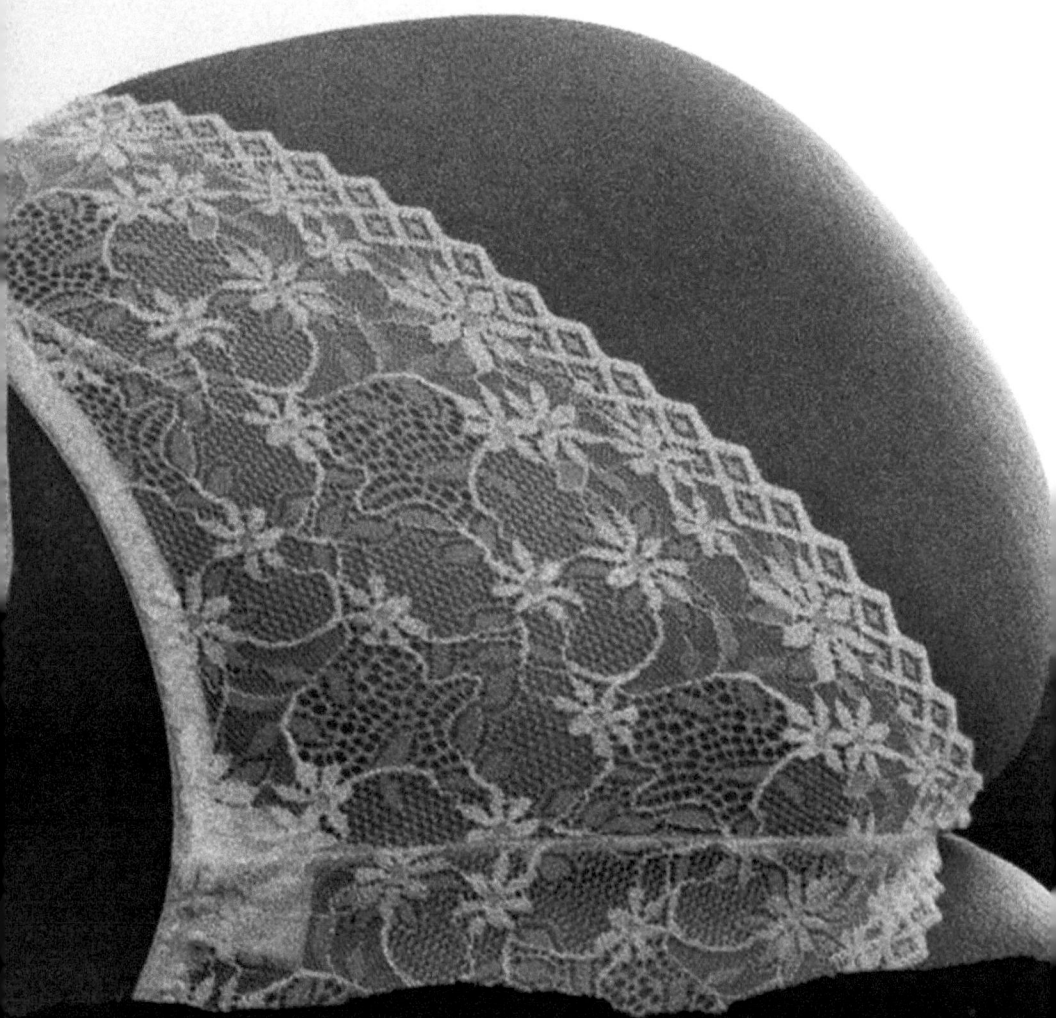

I let myself go with the weight of your body
on top of mine,
I'm bewitched by your fixed stare on me
when you penetrate me slowly, with strength,
with all your desires
all your passion emptied inside of me.
I like to know that I am who I am only with you.
It fascinates me to know that you think I am who I am
not when you embrace me seeking
the woman that only you have met.
I'm impressed with the power of your voice
when you ask me to kiss your whole body.
I like when my ignorant hands fill with knowledge
when caressing your body.
I like who I am when my fingers produce your groans,
I like when you tell me to stop when my tongue
licks your member.
I allow myself to go to unkown places
when on top of you,
when you take me without truce,
without consciousness.
I am filled with pleasure with our nude bodies.
You drive me to discover the limits of my sensuality.
I don't want to distance you from my side,
I dont want to be free of this passion
that makes me insane with lust.

Ghost

The sensation of floating in the air, without direction,
without a destination, allowing the breeze
to carry me slowly, softly, silently.
My light body, without weight, without matter,
without an image, without sound, without scent,
without noise, neither hot nor cold, that must be how
ghosts move around the streets, through the homes,
amongst people, without being perceived or recognized,
unreal, intangible.
Souls with pity that have not been able
to find where to go, where to stay,
who to seek refuge from, lost, disoriented.
I close my eyes and concentrate on my breath
every time I inhale and exhale,
counting the seconds between one and the next,
to assure myself that I am still alive
that I still have not disappeared
from the world that surrounds me.
Sometimes I feel so tenuous, so invisible
that I start to think that I am no longer here, no longer
myself.
How do I realize if my soul has detached from my body,
or ensure myself that due to a misfortune in life,
I am no longer here. I see my body wander amongst
those I love,
I hear my words from a distance in whispers,
but nobody hears them.
No one can see me any longer, nobody can feel me,
no one can perceive me,
because so much lack of love and feelings
have made me unreal, translucent, intangible, invisible.
So much willingness,
so much thought has taken my being,
it's transformed me in the soul with pain that wanders,
dazed through life, desperately seeking love.

I forgot

I forgot what I was before you.
I forgot what I felt before your body possessed mine,
I forgot my own scent before yours impregnated me,
I forgot how I laughed before looking at your smile.
I forgot how to speak until you asked me how I was,
I forgot what I was called until you whispered my name,
I forgot what I ate until you fed me with your words,
I forgot what passion was until you touched me with desperation,
I forgot my daily life when I exchanged it for your fortuitous encounters,
I forgot my own stare until I looked at you,
I forgot I was cold until your arms warmed me.
I forgot that I could fly until I sat atop your wings,
I forgot how to caress until my hands contoured your body.
I forgot pleasure until you kissed me without truce,
I forgot how to surrender until I felt your fingers exploring me,
I forgot how to let my hair down until your hands showed me how,
I forgot how to kiss until I discovered your tongue in my mouth,
I forgot how to dream until you took me away to another world.
I forgot how to look at myself until I saw my reflection in your stare,
I forgot how to walk until I felt your footsteps next to mine,
I forgot all my fantasies until you made love to me.
I forgot how to cry until you left,
I forgot sadness until you did not return,
I forgot melancholy until I started to miss you,
I forgot the pain of heartbreak until I lost you.
I forgot why I no longer wanted to fall in love.

The lover

If I were religious, I would not be writing these words to you. If I were devilish, I would have already bewitched you with my magic potions. If I were decent, I would not have enjoyed your body the way I have been for so long now. If I had been conscious, I would not have heard your convincing words and would not have imagined your hands grabbing my hips.

If I were puritanical, I would not have understood the burning look of desire that penetrated me every time I came to you; I would not have been able to distinguish the rudeness of your passion. If I had been a good woman, I would not be tasting what I find in your mouth at this very moment as I kiss you. If I were demure I would not be smiling as I remember how you stripped me when we meet, every time you take me without warning. If I were shy, I never would have provoked you with my stare with my body and my words. If I were refined, I would not have gone with you the first time that you asked me to. If I were what I should be, I would not be enjoing so much love, so much happiness. If I were respectable, I would not give you some much uncontrolled passion. If I were worried about what people were to say, I wouldn't be sleeping by your side during the day and I wouldn't be kissing you uncontrollably in the middle of the street. I wouldn't be with you when I should be with another…

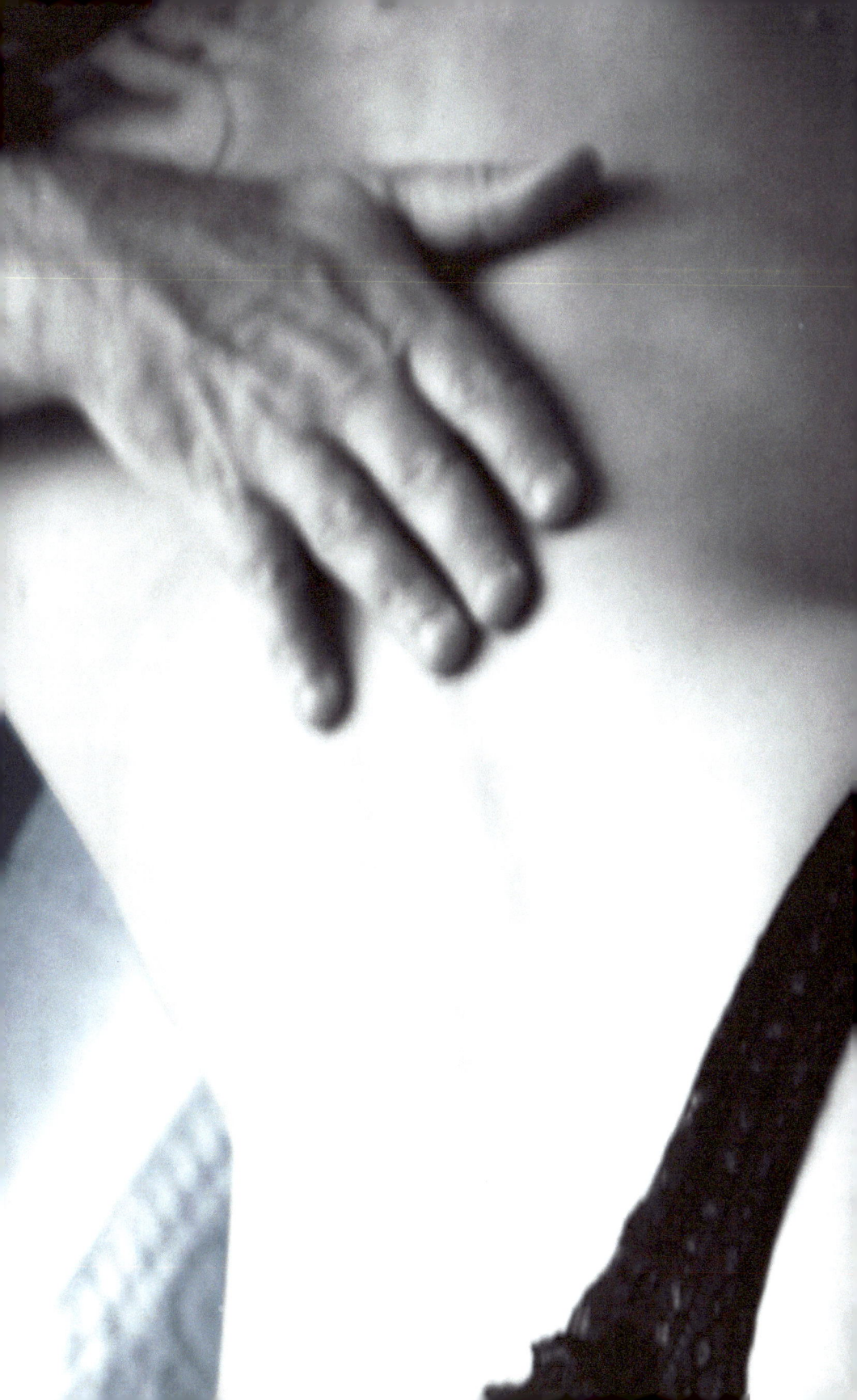

Seeking myself

I don't want to find myself, I'd rather lose myself in who I am, lose myslef in that which I don't know I am, allow myself to be snatched by who I think I am, surrender myself to what I have and have not been. I don't feel like finding the new person within me, but would rather reconcile myself with the one who's always been there with the one that joins me, the one that knows me, that smiles at me and accepts me.

I don't want to reinvent myself, I'm seeking forgiveness from the woman that I've hidden, that I have forgotten, that woman that hasn't seen the light of day in a long time. I want to converse with myself, to ask why and why not, to ask myself where I have been all these years. I want to speak with illusion, with happiness, with patiences, with abandonment, with tolerance, passion, with love and rebelliousness that I carry inside of me.

I don't want to have a new look. I'd rather ask, softly, for the beauty that I have within to show itself, for sensuality to flower from my pores, for my flirtatious nature to invade my eyes, humbly inviting passion to be present on my mouth, on my body, on my hands, on my inside. I would like love to fill me with peace in the deepest of my spirit.

I don't want a lover to pay attention to me, I want to be the one who makes me tremor, to laugh, to feel like a woman. I want it to be me who knows my body, that gives it pleasure, I want it to be me who knows what she wants. I want to surrender myself, without fear, to the woman I have inside me.

Loneliness

Loneliness is the companion of many, it takes over the senses without warning. Loneliness arrives slowly, inoffensive, silently. It mixes with your blood, with your thoughts, with your vital signs, until it's camouflaged within you.

Loneliness betrays you, it tricks you, it's envious and jealous of those who come close to you. Slowly, it becomes indispensable, necessary, needing love and adoration. Without telling you, she smothers you little by little, making your soul feel heavy, presenting you with melancholy, grief, the burden of being alone.

The worst type of loneliness is that which makes you feel that it has left, that life is once again with real people that surround you with warm arms. Loneliness is the emptiness that you find when you are accompanied by someone else who slowly whispers in your ear when everyone else is speaking to you. The one who takes your hand when nobody else does, the one that attachs to your soul because it can sense the cold. There are times when you find it sleeping next to you, when the tears run down your cheeks, and he who sleeps by your side doesn't notice, when you make love and she is the one who dedicates her words of love to you.

Loneliness is your travel companion, when sitting across from him at the table, there are no words, no stares, she is the one that stays with you on Sunday afternoons when everyone is absent. Loneliness is the one who warms your soul when the cold is unbearable, the one that hears your unspoken words, the one that understands emotions that have no meanings for others.

When you let Loneliness into your spirit, to your intimacy, she's faithful, rooted, she takes hold, she stays. Loneliness is the only one that doesn't abandon you, that's persistent, that insists on joining you until the end.

Pity I could not find this antidote in time, now I cannot live without her.

The moon

I look at the moon from my window and I know from the other side of the world you are also looking at the same, me, here, with my loneliness, you there with her company, me here with tears wounding my cheeks, you there kissing her passionately. The same moon, the same sky. Me, here, thinking of you, you there forgetting me. Me, here, loving you… you, there, rejecting me.

Here nightfall is awakening, there it is sleeping, here I await you, you, there, distancing yourself. The night here is cold and I remember when your arms used to warm me. There twilight is warm and your naked body next to hers makes you forget mine. The moon shines sadly on the snow of the mountain, there its reflection is soft on the waves of the sea. I'm here wanting to feel your presence, you're there delighted with hers. I'm here with pain in my soul, you're there happy to have her by your side. The moon makes me dream of that which I do not have, it reminds me of what I've lost, but for you, it gifts to you an evening of love and the happiness it stole from me.

The moon begins to hide behind the clouds, leaving me in the dark and the cold of an unrequited love. There the sun begins to rise, leaving you in the light and warmth of a new day.

In hiding

I hide within my daily routine so I cannot run away, I take on roles that nobody has given to me so I can cease to be me, I entertain myself with daily tasks to forget that I can think, I became critical of others to forget the passions that are suffocating me, I become the shoulder of my companion so I don't become the one seeking empathy, I seek refuge in maternity so I don't free the sinful woman that I have within me, I become religious so I can feel guilty for what I don't feel, I become the beautiful, slim woman in order to hide the sensuous one, the one that was born to give pleasure, I push myself to expend energy in activities to pacify the desires that I cannot satiate, I become a good Samaritan so that they cannot see that I am a sinner, I laugh at everything so they cannot see my tears, I become severe so they cannot notice my wings when I am naked.

My hair always in place, my outfit always correct, without flair, without color. Brand accessories, the cold stones on my hand and the chains around my neck that will not let me flee. The perfect words, all well-thought-out, all controlling the storm that's drowning in my throat. The frozen stare that puts out the fire that burns within me. Hiding myself, for centuries now, cloaked in the security of what is safe.

In reality, I am a sensual, unembarrassed, passionate, free, unleashed, fiery, sinful, turbulent, woman.

Every night my tears fall with forgetfulness, heartbroken, of the lost passion, of unsatisfied desires. Every night, I fall asleep wanting to wake up and be me. I cannot find the courage to let me see me. *Chanel* has won me over.

Goodbye

I don't even know how to say goodbye, I can't get up the courage to get rid of you, I'm not capable of recognizing that you don't feel me anymore, I don't know how to let you go.

My body doesn't allow your departure, my lips cannot pronounce the final word, my heart does not understand that it can beat eventhough you are not here, my eyes cannot see if you do not light the way, my memory cannot erase you, my body goes cool without feeling the heat of yours. My tears do not stop falling when I think that your departure is final.

I drown in anguish of not being able to see you again, weakness invades me completely when I know you are with another, I cannot concentrate on anything when my whole being knows it has been abandoned.

I don't understand why you went away and left me alone with this passion burning inside me, I don't understand why you gave me so much only to take it all away with a goodbye, I can't comprehend how you taught me to love you in a few hours and forgot to tell me how to stop. I can't believe that you left me in a second and abandoned me with the century of pain. It's difficult to understand how you pleased me with so much passion and then ran away without satisfying me completely.

Nobody can satiate the thirst of my mouth as you did, nobody has been able to feed the hunger of my body as you did, no hands have been able to caress my body as yours used to, nobody has been able to make me lose my sense the way you have, I never knew again what it was to hand oneself over unconditionally to someone since I gave it all to you, I never undressed myself the way I did when I was in front of you, my groans never came from my throat again as they did when I was with you. I will never, never feel again what you provoked in me…

Yet, I still have not learned to say goodbye from all that you gave me.

Gratitude

I am grateful to all of those brave people who confided their secrets in me.

To those I left awake with so many questions.

To my husband for not repressing me and loving me for what I am (most of the time).

To the poor mortals that suffered with so much conversation about love.

To my daughters for teaching me to have dreams once again.

To my best friend and soulmate for not judging me.

To all of those that, without knowing it, have been influential in the writings of these lines.

To all those who have witnessed the evolution of this woman, and still continue to love me.

But above all, I'm grateful for the wonderful rebel that I have within me to remind me of who I am.

Blanca Urquhart Eyzaguirre, was born in Santiago, Chile, July 20, 1964. From an early age, she developed a passion for writing and reading. Her vivid imagination, frequent doubts and rebellious spirit could not find a place in the conservative atmosphere of Chilean society. As soon as she had finished her degree in Communications, she left to seek adventure in distant lands hoping to find freedom to think, to be herself, and love without being judged.

In the last few years, she has lived in diverse countries with her husband and two daughters, which has allowed her to gather stories for her writings and friends for her conversations. She had embraced other cultures, discovering new flavors, colors and Gods. Chile, however, continues to be her anchor, especially her beloved Futaleufu in Chilean Patagonia.

She currently resides in France where she decided to publish *Curves of the Soul*.

www.ingramcontent.com/pod-product-compliance
Lightning Source LLC
Chambersburg PA
CBHW042129080426
42735CB00001B/14